WORLD'S MOST
DANGEROUS
ANIMALS

ſilʋer draǧoɲ books

World's Most Dangerous Animals, March 2012. First Printing. Published by Silver Dragon Books, Inc., 433 Caredean Drive, Ste. C, Horsham, Pennsylvania 19044. Silver Dragon Books and its logos are ® and © 2012 Silver Dragon Books, Inc. All Rights Reserved.

WRITERS
JOE BRUSHA, NEO EDMUND, ROBERT GREENBERGER, BARBARA KESEL,
PAUL KUPPERBERG, AARON ROSENBERG AND DARREN VINCENZO
ARTISTS
SPACE GOAT'S BLANCO-JOK, CARMEN NUNEZ CARNERO, DSAGAR FORNIES,
SPACE GOAT'S GERVASIO-BRABO-MALLEA, GORDON PURCELL,
MATTHEW REYNOLDS AND ALESSANDRO VENTURA
COLORIST
SPACE GOAT'S BLANCO-JOK
LETTERER
JIM CAMPBELL
COVER
STEAMBOT STUDIOS
PRODUCTION
CHRISTOPHER COTE

SPECIAL THANKS TO
ELIZABETH BAKACS, MINDY BARSKY,
GRANT MCALLISTER, BRIDGET STOYKO,
TOM MASON AND MARCIO FREIRE

PUBLISHER
JOE BRUSHA
EDITOR
BOB GREENBERGER
LICENSING & BUSINESS DEVELOPMENT
JENNIFER BERMEL

PUBLISHED BY
SILVER DRAGON BOOKS
433 CAREDEAN DRIVE, STE. C
HORSHAM, PA 19044
WWW.SILVERDRAGONBOOKS.COM

FIRST PRINTING
ISBN: 978-0-9827507-3-5

ANIMAL
PLANET

WORLD'S MOST DANGEROUS ANIMALS

INTRODUCTION

The closest most of us ever get to see a wild animal, other than the common squirrel or rabbit, is from outside the safety of the cages at our local zoo. Most people go their entire life without seeing a bear in its natural habitat let alone a lion or a hippo. As man has spread across the globe the habitats of wild animals have become smaller and smaller, pushing dangerous animals out of contact with all but a small number of people.

But there are still wild places in the world where danger still lurks... places where occasionally man finds himself playing the role of the hunted as opposed to the hunter. Like the African savanna where the king of the jungle, the African lion, stalks its prey... prey that every so often includes man.

The rivers and billabongs of Australia are home to the largest predatory reptile on the planet, the Salt Water Crocodile. Anyone taking a swim in the wild waters of Australia needs to be wary of this living relic of the dinosaur age. Even in places like North America, there are areas where animals still reign. In the mountains and forests of the Pacific Northwest two ton Grizzly Bears walk the same paths as hikers, hunters and campers.

Most of us will never meet one of these animals face to face in the wild. But for those of us who do, we can only hope that the one we meet takes no interest in us. Even though man has come to dominate the planet, we are still no match for the raw power of nature. And we don't stand a chance when we meet the World's Most Dangerous Animals.

CAPE BUFFALO

ANY ANIMAL FOOLISH ENOUGH TO ATTACK THE CAPE BUFFALO HAS TO DEAL WITH ITS SHARP HORNS THAT MEASURE NEARLY THREE FEET ACROSS.

FACT FILE

AVERAGE HEIGHT: 5.5 FEET

AVERAGE WEIGHT: 1,400–2,000 LBS

LENGTH: 11 FEET

COLOR: REDDISH BROWN TO DARK BROWN OR BLACK.

HABITAT: AFRICAN SWAMPS, FLOODPLAINS, GRASSLANDS, AND RAIN FORESTS.

DIET: HERBIVORE, GRAZES ON GRASS AND LOCAL PLANTS.

PREDATORS: LIONS ARE THEIR GREATEST DANGER BUT IT USUALLY TAKES MORE THAN ONE ATTACKER TO BRING DOWN A CAPE BUFFALO.

DISPOSITION: EXTREMELY TERRITORIAL AND AGGRESSIVE.

HUMAN ATTACKS PER YEAR: 200+

ITS THICK HIDE IS SO TOUGH THAT WOULD-BE PREDATORS SLIDE RIGHT OFF. EVEN A LION WOULDN'T RISK AN ATTACK.

COUPLED WITH ITS MASSIVE TREE-TRUNK LEGS THE CAPE BUFFALO IS PERFECTLY ARMED TO CRUSH AND MANGLE ANYONE OR ANYTHING IN ITS WAY.

LOCALS SAY THE BEAST IS SO FIERCELY TERRITORIAL THAT IT

DID YOU KNOW?

POSSIBLY SECOND ONLY TO THE ELEPHANT, CAPE BUFFALOES ARE KNOWN FOR THEIR **MEMORIES**.

AS A RESULT, THEY HOLD **GRUDGES** AND WILL ATTACK A RIVAL **YEARS** AFTER THE FIRST ALTERCATION.

OR, THEY **REMEMBER** THOSE WHO HAVE BEEN **GOOD** TO THEM AND DEMAND **AFFECTION** WHEN NEXT THEY MEET.

AFRICAN ELEPHANT

BOTH MALES AND FEMALES HAVE TUSKS, WHICH ARE USED FOR DIGGING, MARKING OF TERRITORY, AND DEFENSE AGAINST PREDATORS.

AN ELEPHANT'S TRUNK HAS HUNDREDS OF THOUSANDS OF INDIVIDUAL MUSCLES, MAKING THIS APPENDAGE A VERSATILE TOOL USED FOR BREATHING, SMELLING, EATING, DRINKING, GRABBING AND COMMUNICATING.

ELEPHANTS HAVE AMONG THE LARGEST AND MOST DEVELOPED BRAINS IN THE ANIMAL KINGDOM. THEIR MEMORIES ARE QUITE ACUTE AND BUILT AROUND SKILLS NEEDED FOR SURVIVAL.

FACT FILE

AVERAGE HEIGHT: 8-13 FEET AT THE SHOULDER

AVERAGE WEIGHT: 3-8 TONS

HABITAT: AFRICAN SAVANNAH BUSH LANDS OR WESTERN FORESTS.

DIET: HERBIVORE, FOOD INCLUDES GRASSES, LEAVES, BARK, FRUIT, TWIGS, SEED PODS, ROOTS.

PREDATORS: LIONS AND TIGERS. HYENAS WILL SOMETIMES ATTACK A VERY YOUNG ELEPHANT.

BEHAVIORAL PATTERN: HERDS CONGREGATE NEAR SOURCES OF WATER, THEN ROAM FOR FORAGE. YOUNG BULLS LEAVE THE HERD AT PUBERTY, EITHER STAYING SOLITARY OR FORMING ALL-MALE HERDS.

HUMAN ATTACKS PER YEAR: 300-500

FWAM

STAY CALM! SHE IS *PROTECTING* HER HERD. JUST REMAIN *STILL.*

IT'S... SCARED?

SERIOUSLY, IT LOOKED SCARED.

GRIZZLY BEAR

THE GRIZZLY, ALSO KNOWN AS THE SILVERTIP BEAR, IS A SUB-SPECIES OF THE NORTH AMERICAN BROWN BEAR.

FACT FILE

AVERAGE HEIGHT: 3.5 FEET AT THE SHOULDERS; 7 FEET TALL STANDING

AVERAGE WEIGHT: 500-1,000 LBS

TOP SPEED: 35 MPH

LARGEST RECORDED: IN ALASKA, 12.5 FEET TALL AND 1,600 LBS.

HABITAT: CANADA, NORTHWESTERN UNITED STATES, ALASKA.

DIET: LARGE MAMMALS LIKE MOOSE, DEER AND SHEEP, FISH, PLANTS.

HUMAN ATTACKS PER YEAR: 2

A SOLITARY HUNTER BY NATURE, THE GRIZZLY IS ONE OF THE LARGEST PREDATORY ANIMALS IN NORTH AMERICA.

GRIZZLY BEAR CLAWS ARE LONG, CURVED, EXCEPTIONALLY SHARP, AND USED AS DIGGING AND HUNTING TOOLS.

WHEN I HAD FIRST COME UP HERE TO LIVE IN THE ALASKAN WILDERNESS LATE LAST YEAR, JUST ABOUT THE ONLY THING ANYONE THOUGHT TO WARN ME ABOUT WAS THE **GRIZZLY BEARS.**

I WAS ASSURED THAT THE CHANCES OF BEING **ATTACKED** BY ONE OF THESE ALMOST ONE-HALF TON CARNIVORES WAS **SLIGHT** ... BUT THAT I SHOULD ALWAYS KEEP A GUN **HANDY.**

THE BEST ADVICE WAS, AS LONG AS I KEPT FOOD IN **SEALED** CONTAINERS AND MY CAMP CLEAR OF TRASH, THE GRIZZLIES WOULD WANT AS LITTLE TO DO WITH ME AS I DID WITH THEM.

THAT TURNED OUT TO BE GOOD ADVICE ... UNTIL THE LATE-SUMMER, WHEN I WAS WASHING UP IN THE RIVER THAT RAN BY MY CABIN.

UP UNTIL THEN, I HAD SEEN A FEW BEARS BUT ONLY FROM A **DISTANCE**.

GRIZZLY BEARS ARE VERY TERRITORIAL, **LONERS** BY NATURE, AND IN CONFRONTATIONS WITH OTHER SPECIES, THEY'RE USUALLY THE **AGGRESSORS**.

AND IT'S EASY TO SEE WHY! AS ONE OF NORTH AMERICA'S LARGEST PREDATORS, THE GRIZZLY BEAR HAS FEW RIVALS.

AS SOON AS HE CAUGHT MY **SCENT**, THE BIG GRIZZLY TOOK OFF, BACK INTO THE WOODS HE'D COME FROM.

I WAS RELIEVED, BELIEVING THAT MY TERRIFYING BUT **BRIEF** ENCOUNTER WAS OVER ALMOST AS SOON AS IT HAD STARTED.

BUT IT WASN'T.

THE GRIZZLY BEAR IS TAILOR-MADE FOR HUNTING. *URSUS ARCTOS HORRIBILIS* IS BIG, POWERFUL, AND **FAST**!

HE LIVES IN WOODLANDS, FORESTS, MEADOWS, VALLEYS, AND NEAR RIVERS AND STREAMS, WHEREVER **FOOD** IS AVAILABLE.

HIS SENSE OF SMELL IS AS ACUTE AS HIS EYESIGHT IS **POOR**, BUT ONCE THE GRIZZLY GETS THE **SCENT**, HE STALKS HIS PREY WITH STEALTH AND CUNNING.

TODAY, THEY CAN BE FOUND ONLY IN ALASKA, THE NORTHWESTERN U.S., AND, MOST ABUNDANTLY, IN CANADA.

GRIZZLY BEARS ONCE RANGED FROM ALASKA TO MEXICO AND ACROSS NORTH AMERICA, TO HUDSON'S BAY IN NORTHEASTERN CANADA.

THE GRIZZLY CAN RUN AT SPEEDS OF UP TO **35 MPH** ...

... AND A **MAN**, AT HIS BEST, IS AROUND **27 MPH**!

WITH THESE, GRIZZLIES CAN RIP OPEN THE SOFT UNDERBELLY OF ITS PREY AND WILL BEGIN TO EAT IT ALIVE.

IT'S SAID THAT BEING KILLED BY A GRIZZLY IS SLOW AND HORRIBLY PAINFUL!

IN LATE SUMMER AND EARLY AUTUMN, AFTER THE MATING SEASON, GRIZZLIES BEGIN TO STORE UP FAT AND PROTEIN FOR THE COMING WINTER HIBERNATION.

IT IS DURING HIBERNATION, IN DENS AT HIGH ELEVATIONS, THAT MOTHER GRIZZLIES BEGIN THEIR REPRODUCTIVE CYCLES.

GRIZZLIES WILL SLEEP THE WINTER AWAY, FEEDING OFF THEIR BODIES RESERVES DURING THE SEASON WHEN GAME IS SCARCE.

THOUGH IMPREGNATED DURING THE SUMMER, THE FEMALE DELAYS IMPLANTING THE EMBRYO UNTIL HIBERNATION!

THE GRIZZLY HAS ONE OF THE LOWEST REPRODUCTIVE RATES OF ANY NORTH AMERICAN LAND MAMMAL. FEMALES AVERAGE TWO CUBS IN A LITTER.

IT TAKES GRIZZLIES FIVE YEARS TO REACH SEXUAL MATURITY, AND MOTHERS DO NOT MATE DURING THE TWO YEARS THEY CARE FOR THEIR CUBS.

THE BEAR CHARGED AND, BEFORE I COULD GET A CLEAR AIM, HE DISAPPEARED INTO THE WOODS.

BUT HE WASN'T LEAVING. I COULD HEAR THE GRIZZLY THRASHING AROUND IN THE UNDERBRUSH, COMING CLOSER.

AND THEN HE WAS ON TOP OF ME, AN 800-POUND MOUNTAIN OF MUSCLE AND FUR!

MY ATTACKER QUICKLY LOST INTEREST IN MY LIMP, MOTIONLESS BODY.

I WAS LUCKIER THAN MANY OTHER VICTIMS OF GRIZZLY BEARS...

...ALTHOUGH I SUFFERED SEVERE LACERATIONS AND BROKEN BONES, I HAD **LIVED** TO TELL THE STORY!

HIPPOPOTAMUS

A HIPPO CAN OPEN ITS MOUTH MORE THAN THREE FEET WIDE AND ITS TEETH AND CANINES NEVER STOP GROWING. THE TUSKS ARE AT THE FRONT OF THE MOUTH AND ARE MAINLY USED FOR FIGHTING OFF PREDATORS AND RIVAL HIPPOS AND ARE CAPABLE OF BITING A SMALL BOAT IN HALF.

A HIPPO'S FOOT HAS FOUR TOES WITH MEMBRANES BETWEEN EACH WHICH ALLOWS IT TO MOVE DEFTLY IN WATER. THEY ALSO SPLAY OUT TO DISTRIBUTE WEIGHT EVENLY AND TO SUPPORT THIS MASSIVE QUADRUPED ON LAND.

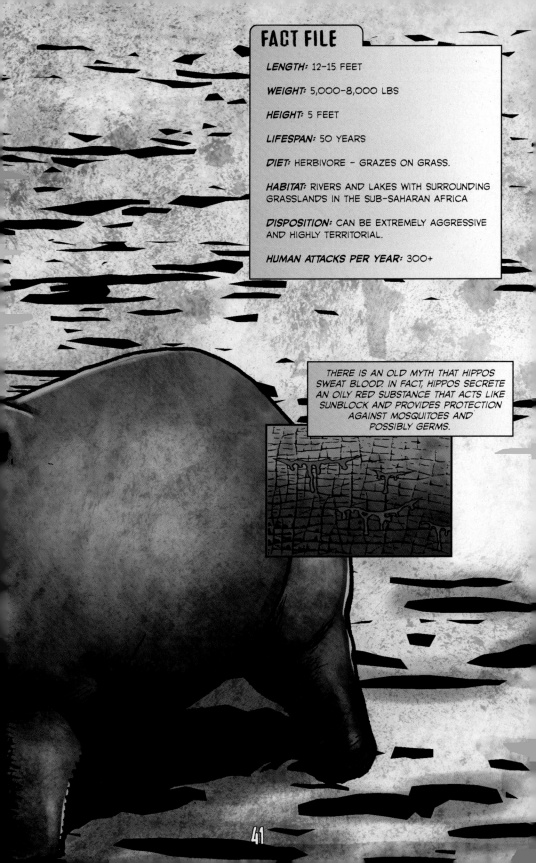

FACT FILE

LENGTH: 12-15 FEET

WEIGHT: 5,000-8,000 LBS

HEIGHT: 5 FEET

LIFESPAN: 50 YEARS

DIET: HERBIVORE - GRAZES ON GRASS.

HABITAT: RIVERS AND LAKES WITH SURROUNDING GRASSLANDS IN THE SUB-SAHARAN AFRICA

DISPOSITION: CAN BE EXTREMELY AGGRESSIVE AND HIGHLY TERRITORIAL.

HUMAN ATTACKS PER YEAR: 300+

THERE IS AN OLD MYTH THAT HIPPOS SWEAT BLOOD. IN FACT, HIPPOS SECRETE AN OILY RED SUBSTANCE THAT ACTS LIKE SUNBLOCK AND PROVIDES PROTECTION AGAINST MOSQUITOES AND POSSIBLY GERMS.

AFRICA ... FOR OVER A CENTURY IT WAS KNOWN BY WESTERNERS AS THE *"DARK CONTINENT."*

THE **LURE** OF ADVENTURE LED MANY EARLY EXPLORERS TO BRAVE THIS MYSTERIOUS AND **HOSTILE** WORLD.

SOME CAME IN SEARCH OF **FORTUNE** AND **GLORY** ...

... OTHERS ON A QUEST FOR **KNOWLEDGE**. AFRICA WAS FILLED WITH INNUMERABLE **NEW** SPECIES OF ANIMALS ALONG WITH **UNEXPLORED** TERRITORIES NEVER BEFORE SEEN BY WESTERN MAN.

MANY EXPLORERS SET OUT TO CHART AND MAP THOSE **UNKNOWN TERRITORIES** AND **RECORD** NEW TYPES OF ANIMAL SPECIES.

NOT **ALL** OF THOSE NEW SPECIES WERE **HAPPY** TO BE DISCOVERED.

EARLY EXPLORERS **SOON** FOUND OUT HOW **DANGEROUS** HIPPOS COULD BE IN THE **WATER.**

AFRICAN NATIVES KNEW THAT THEY COULD BE EVEN **MORE** DANGEROUS ON **LAND.**

RUSTLE RUSTLE

WHEN **CUT OFF** FROM THE WATER OR ...

WHEN THEY HAVE **YOUNG** NEARBY ...

... HIPPOS ARE AMONG THE MOST **DANGEROUS** AND DEADLY ANIMALS ON THE ENTIRE **PLANET.**

HIPPOS CAN WEIGH UP TO 8,000 POUNDS.

THEY CAN EASILY RUN AT 18 MILES PER HOUR.

AND THEIR CANINE TEETH, MORE LIKE HUGE TUSKS, CAN GROW UP TO THREE FEET IN LENGTH.

THIS ANIMAL IS ANYTHING BUT CUTE AND CUDDLY.

IN AFRICA IT IS ESTIMATED THAT MORE PEOPLE ARE KILLED BY HIPPOS EVERY YEAR THAN ALL OTHER ANIMAL-CAUSED DEATHS COMBINED.

THE HIPPO'S *OUTWARD* APPEARANCE HIDES ITS *AGGRESSIVE* AND *DANGEROUS* NATURE.

THEY ARE FIERCELY *TERRITORIAL* BOTH IN THE WATER AND OUT.

IT SEEMS THAT ANYONE WHO TRAVELS RIVERS POPULATED BY *HIPPOS* NEEDS TO TAKE EXTRA *CARE.*

IN 2003, *DIANA TILDEN-DAVIS,* A FORMER *MISS SOUTH AFRICA,* WAS CANOEING IN THE OKAVANGO SWAMPS OF *BOTSWANA* WHEN SHE ENCOUNTERED A *HIPPO* ...

THIS POPULAR TOURIST LOCATION HAS A THRIVING HIPPO POPULATION, WHICH HAS NO *LOVE* FOR CANOES *OR* THEIR PASSENGERS.

ONE OF THE HIPPOS APPROACHED DIANA'S CANOE...

THE FORMER PAGEANT QUEEN WAS *LUCKY* TO ESCAPE WITH HER *LIFE.*

A MONTH EARLIER, A WOMA[N] *DIED* IN A SIMILAR ATTACK [AT] THE *SAME* LOCATION.

ONE OF THE *CUTEST* AND MOST *POPULA[R]* ATTRACTIONS AT ZOOS AROUND THE WORL[D] THE HIPPOPOTAMUS IS PERHAPS THE MOS[T] *DANGEROUS* OF *ALL* ANIMALS WHEN ENCOUNTERED IN ITS *NATURAL* HABITAT.

DID YOU KNOW?

SEMI-AQUATIC, HIPPOPOTAMUSES SPEND THEIR DAYS COOLING OFF IN THE WATER BEFORE HEADING OUT AT DUSK IN SEARCH OF *FOOD*.

THE COOL RIVER WATER HELPS THEM CONSERVE ENERGY. IF THERE IS *INSUFFICIENT* WATER, THEY WILL COVER THEMSELVES IN *MUD* FOR *PROTECTION* FROM THE SUN. *MATING* AND GIVING *BIRTH* ALSO OCCUR IN THE *WATER*.

KING COBRA

THE KING COBRA'S FANGS ARE A HALF-INCH IN LENGTH. THEY CAN PIERCE THROUGH FLESH AND INJECT LETHAL VENOM LIKE A HYPODERMIC NEEDLE.

FACT FILE

AVERAGE HEIGHT: 18–20 FEET

AVERAGE WEIGHT: 30–40 LBS

COLOR: OLIVE, BROWN AND BLACK.

HABITAT: DENSE HIGHLAND FORESTS, NEAR LAKES AND RIVERS OF INDIA, SOUTHERN CHINA AND SOUTHEAST ASIA.

DIET: PRIMARILY EATS OTHER SNAKES, BUT WILL ALSO EAT FROGS, LIZARDS AND SMALL MAMMALS LIKE RODENTS AND RABBITS.

PREDATORS: LARGE BIRDS OF PREY AND MONGOOSES.

DISPOSITION: AGGRESSIVE. FEARLESS. WILL STAND UP TO ANY ENEMY AND CAN EVEN TAKE DOWN AN ADULT ELEPHANT.

HUMAN ATTACKS PER YEAR: 2,000

WHEN THE KING COBRA IS THREATENED OR PREPARED TO ATTACK, IT FLATTENS ITS NECK RIBS TO FORM A HOOD AROUND ITS HEAD...

...THIS GIVES IT A DANGEROUS AND MENACING APPEARANCE TO INSTILL FEAR IN ITS ENEMIES.

THE JAW BONES ARE CONNECTED BY PLIABLE LIGAMENTS, ENABLING THE LOWER JAW TO OPEN WIDE ENOUGH TO SWALLOW ITS PREY WHOLE...

...AND USUALLY WHILE IT IS STILL ALIVE.

FOR THE PEOPLE OF KING COBRA VILLAGE DEEP IN THE HEART OF THAILAND, DEALING WITH DANGEROUS SNAKES IS VERY COMMON.

FROM A VERY YOUNG AGE THE MEN TRAIN IN THE ART OF SPARRING WITH THE DEADLY REPTILES.

THE KING COBRA IS THE LONGEST VENOMOUS SNAKE IN THE WORLD.

A SINGLE BITE CAN KILL AN ELEPHANT IN A FEW HOURS.

...OR A MAN IN ONLY MINUTES.

IT IS THE ONLY SNAKE THAT WILL PROTECT ITS NEST AFTER LAYING EGGS...

...BUT IT WILL NOT STAY AROUND AFTER THE HATCHLINGS ARE BORN...

THE COBRA IS A CANNIBAL THAT LOVES TO EAT OTHER SNAKES.

IT WILL NOT THINK TWICE TO FEAST ON ITS OWN YOUNG.

GATHERING FRUIT IS FOR LITTLE *CHILDREN*. I SHOULD BE IN THE VILLAGE WITH *FATHER* SPARRING WITH *COBRAS*.

FORGET ABOUT IT. LET'S CLIMB THAT *TREE* AND GET SOME *MANGOSTEENS*.

IF *I* CAME FACE TO FACE WITH A COBRA *RIGHT NOW* I WOULD SHOW IT I'M *NOT* AFRAID.

NO *WAY*. YOU WOULD RUN *HOME CRYING* TO MOMMY!

DON'T *WORRY*, YOU COWARD. *NOTHING* IS GOING TO HAPPEN.

THESE ARE TOO *SMALL*. THE *BIGGER* ONES ARE AT THE *TOP*.

YOU'RE *CRAZY!* THE BRANCHES UP THERE WON'T *HOLD* US.

ALMOST GOT IT!

WHOA!

CREAKKK

PANG HAS SPOTTED A KING COBRA IN A *FIERCE* BATTLE AGAINST ANOTHER VENOMOUS SNAKE CALLED A *MANGROVE*.

THE MANGROVE IS MERELY FIGHTING FOR ITS *LIFE*, BUT THE KING COBRA IS ON THE HUNT FOR A QUICK *MEAL*.

WHILE THE MANGROVE IS A *DANGEROUS* SNAKE, THE KING COBRA IS FAR QUICKER... AND *DEADLY*.

THE COBRA DOESN'T *WAIT* FOR THE DEFEATED MANGROVE TO *STOP* BREATHING...

THE KING COBRA INJECTS THE MANGROVE WITH ITS DEADLY VENOM.

...BEFORE SWALLOWING IT *WHOLE*.

DAD. I'M SO *SORRY.*

I'LL BE OKAY. I'M *PROUD* OF YOU TWO FOR BEING SO *BRAVE.*

HE'S BEEN *BITTEN.* PLEASE *HURRY!*

THIS *ANTI-VENOM* SHOULD *SAVE* HIM. IF WE'RE NOT *TOO LATE.*

I AM *NOT* AFRAID. I BELIEVE HE *WILL* BE OKAY.

SEVERAL WEEKS LATER.

THANKS TO A QUICK INJECTION OF ANTI-VENOM, THE KING COBRA'S BITE WASN'T *FATAL*.

OVER **ONE MILLION PEOPLE** EVERY YEAR ARE **BITTEN** BY VENOMOUS SNAKES.

OF THOSE OVER **125,000** OF THEM LOSE THEIR **LIVES**.

WHILE THE **DANGER** IS CLEAR, FOR THE **FEARLESS** MEN OF KING COBRA VILLAGE, THE TRADITION OF SPARRING WITH THESE **DEADLY REPTILES** LIVES ON EACH AND EVERY **DAY**...

KOMODO DRAGON

FACT FILE

AVERAGE HEIGHT: 7-10 FEET

AVERAGE WEIGHT: 120-160 LBS

HABITAT: TROPCAL SAVANNAH AND FORESTS, BUT RANGE WIDELY FROM BEACHES TO ROCKY RIDGES AND ARE ONLY FOUND ON THE ISLANDS OF KOMODO.

DIET: CARNIVORE, ANYTHING FROM RODENTS TO DEER TO WATER BUFFALO. THEY WILL ALSO FEED ON THE CARCASSES OF DEAD ANIMALS.

HUNTING METHOD: AMBUSH. THEY LIE IN WAIT FOR PREY.

HUMAN ATTACKS PER YEAR: <1

MUCH LIKE A SNAKE, THE KOMODO DRAGON USES A FORKED TONGUE TO "TASTE" THE AIR AND DETECT PREY, AS WELL AS LOCATE CARRION (DEAD ANIMALS) FROM UP TO 2 ½ MILES AWAY!

THE KOMODO DRAGON'S TEETH ARE SERRATED AND POINT TOWARDS THE BACK OF ITS MOUTH, TO KEEP PREY FROM ESCAPING ITS GRIP. ITS SALIVA IS LACED WITH OVER FIFTY STRAINS OF DEADLY BACTERIA AND RECENT EVIDENCE INDICATES THE DRAGONS SECRETE LETHAL VENOM AS WELL.

THE KOMODO IS ARMED WITH SHARP, CURVED CLAWS, WHICH IT USES TO DISEMBOWEL ITS VICTIMS, RESULTING IN HEAVY BLOOD LOSS AND QUICK DEATH. THOUGH IT DOESN'T APPEAR TO BE BUILT FOR SPEED, THE DRAGON CAN SPRINT IN SHORT BURSTS UP TO 13 MILES PER HOUR!

STORIES OF **DRAGONS** HAVE BEEN TOLD IN MANY CULTURES SINCE BEFORE RECORDED HISTORY. IN THE FAR EAST, THE DRAGON HAS COME TO SYMBOLIZE **POWER** AND **MAJESTY.**

IN THE EARLY YEARS OF THE 20th CENTURY, PEARL DIVERS IN INDONESIA BROUGHT BACK STORIES OF "LAND CROCODILES" AND DESCRIPTIONS OF **FEARSOME** CREATURES ROAMING THE **SUNDA ISLANDS.**

IN 1910, A DUTCHMAN NAMED **J.K. VAN STEYN VAN HENSBROEK** BROUGHT ACTUAL **EVIDENCE** OF THE EXISTENCE OF THESE CREATURES TO THE WESTERN WORLD. PHOTOS AND SKINS LED TO THE PUBLICATION OF A SCIENTIFIC PAPER ON THE **"DRAGON LIZARD."**

IN THE EARLY HOURS OF A JUNE MORNING IN 1926, AN EXPEDITION SANCTIONED BY THE **AMERICAN MUSEUM OF NATURAL HISTORY,** AND LED BY **W. DOUGLAS BURDEN,** REACHED THE ISLAND OF KOMODO IN THE SUNDA ISLANDS OF INDONESIA.

DURING WHAT ULTIMATELY WOULD BECOME THE INSPIRATION FOR THE 1933 MOVIE **KING KONG,** BURDEN WOULD BE THE FIRST TO CAPTURE A **LIVING** KOMODO DRAGON, BEGINNING AN AMERICAN FASCINATION WITH THE WORLD'S **LARGEST** REPTILE.

IN HIS 1927 BOOK, **DRAGON LIZARDS OF KOMODO**, W. DOUGLAS BURDEN WROTE:

We seemed to see a prehistoric landscape -- a lost world -- unfold before us. it is a melancholy land, a suitable haunt for the predatory dragon lizards.

Along with Mrs. Burden, I was accompanied by my good friend F.J. Defosse, and the esteemed herpetologist, Dr. E.R. Dunn. Rounding out our group was a Chinese cameraman by the name of Lee Fei, and fifteen Malays.

WHILE THE GROUP SAW MANY SIGNS OF THEIR QUARRY, BURDEN DID NOT MEET THE INFAMOUS "DRAGON LIZARD" UNTIL THEIR THIRD DAY ON KOMODO ISLAND.

At the foot of a gentle slope, I saw my first Dragon. He was a monster -- huge, noble and ancient. it was a perfectly marvelous sight -- a primeval monster in a primeval setting -- sufficient to give any hunter the thrill of a lifetime.

He walked slowly and sedately along, obviously hunting for something, his yellow tongue working incessantly, his magnificent head swinging ponderously this way and that.

Thus began our study of these magnificent creatures. They are opportunistic carnivores, feeding on a wide variety of prey.

AS HATCHLINGS OR SMALL ADULTS, KOMODO DRAGONS WILL EAT INSECTS, LIZARDS, RATS, EGGS, BIRDS, AND CARRION.

LARGE ADULTS WILL PROWL GAME TRAILS AND LIE IN WAIT TO ATTACK WILD BOAR, DEER, WATER BUFFALO, AND EVEN EACH OTHER.

The dragon lizard sat motionless on the edge of the jungle, watching a buffalo that trotted unsuspectingly toward him.

A KOMODO ATTACK IS *SWIFT* AND *LETHAL*. IT WILL LATCH ONTO ITS PREY, USUALLY KNOCKING IT TO THE GROUND. ITS STRONG MUSCLES, POWERFUL *JAWS*, RAZOR-SHARP *TEETH* AND SAVAGE *CLAWS* MAKE SHORT WORK OF ITS VICTIM.

THE SALIVA OF THE KOMODO CONTAINS OVER *FIFTY STRAINS* OF VIRULENT BACTERIA. SHOULD AN ANIMAL SOMEHOW ESCAPE THE DRAGON'S JAWS, THESE BACTERIA CERTAINLY WOULD CONTRIBUTE TO ITS *DEATH*.

HOWEVER, IT WAS DISCOVERED IN 2009 THAT THE KOMODO DRAGON ALSO PRODUCES A *VENOM* WHOSE *TOXINS* CAUSE ITS VICTIM TO GO INTO *SHOCK* AND INHIBIT THE *CLOTTING* OF BLOOD.

NEITHER THE VENOM NOR THE BACTERIA SEEM TO HAVE *ANY* AFFECT ON OTHER *KOMODOS*, HOWEVER.

FREQUENT CLASHES BETWEEN DRAGONS RESULT IN MANY BATTLE SCARS BUT ONLY AN OCCASIONAL DEATH.

BATTLES MAY BE WAGED OVER FOOD, MATES AND TERRITORY.

AFTER PINNING HIS ADVERSARY, TO THE VICTOR BELONG THE SPOILS.

The recurved teeth with serrated edges are employed to rip off great chunks of the foul meat. The beast maneuvers this by seesawing back and forth on braced legs, giving a wrench with every backward move.

WHILE VERY LARGE PREY IS TORN TO PIECES, KOMODO DRAGONS CAN SWALLOW HUGE CHUNKS OF MEAT BY FORCING IT INTO THEIR MOUTHS.

THEIR FLEXIBLE JAWS, MADE UP OF SEVERAL MOVABLE JOINTS, CAN OPEN UNUSUALLY WIDE AND MOVE FORWARD TO ENGULF IT. A LARGE DRAGON CAN SWALLOW THE ENTIRE HINDQUARTERS OF AN ADULT DEER!

AFTER EATING AS MUCH AS **80%** OF ITS OWN WEIGHT IN MEAT, THE DRAGON DRAGS ITSELF TO A SUNNY SPOT TO SLOWLY **DIGEST** ITS MEAL. BECAUSE OF ITS SLOW METABOLISM, A LARGE DRAGON CAN SURVIVE ON AS FEW AS **TWELVE MEALS** A YEAR.

Later, when we reached the backbone of the island, from the crest we could look down on all sides, to a blood-red, sunlit sea dotted here and there with islands of indescribable shape and beauty.

Never was night more enchanting. The spirit of the place came with every breath of air that stroked those ancient hills, and with it a pleasurable feeling of how little importance here is man.

The next day we were on the job early in the morning. Our goal was to capture one of these magnificent creatures. Under Defosse's direction, we constructed leafy screens, or "bomas", from which we could observe the lizards.

THE LIZARD'S LARGE SIZE IS DUE TO **ISLAND GIGANTISM,** SINCE IT IS THE **LARGEST** PREDATOR IN ITS ENVIRONMENT, AS WELL AS ITS **SLOW** METABOLISM.

ISLAND GIGANTISM OR INSULAR GIANTISM IS A BIOLOGICAL PHENOMENON IN WHICH THE SIZE OF ANIMALS ISOLATED ON AN ISLAND INCREASES DRAMATICALLY IN COMPARISON TO THEIR MAINLAND RELATIVES.

Defosse devised an ingenious spring trap, using a strong tree bent low to the ground and fastened down. A hidden release, triggered when the monster lunges for the bait, jerks the beast aloft.

For a long time we waited in the boma. Suddenly one of the men made a strange sound. On peeping through the back of the boma, I saw a dragon -- a living remnant of the Pleistocene.

He passed right by on one side of the boma. I could have reached out and touched him with my hand. I had the tingling sensation of actually having a dragon walk within a yard of where I was standing!

Then it happened.

The monster took the bait.

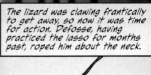

The lizard was clawing frantically to get away, so now it was time for action. Defosse, having practiced the lasso for months past, roped him about the neck.

The trap was triggered and the dragon found himself sailing into the air. However, at the same moment, there was a terrible cracking.

As the rope tightened, the spring pole cracked and bent at the point of breakage. Instead of being suspended in the air, our prize was on the ground, tugging at the tether.

A third rope was thrown about the tail. We had our prize!

We were well satisfied with our work, and made our way back to where The Dog lay waiting for us at anchor.

Our collections complete, we were ready to return home. Of the Varanus Komodensis, we took two live adult specimens, and twelve dead; fourteen in all.

In a very short time, we were sailing away from one of the most charming and romantic islands in the world. With deep regret we left Komodo's lonely shores behind, a great shadow looming weird and indefinite in the distance.

AFRICAN LION

LIONS LIVE IN GROUPS CALLED PRIDES. A PRIDE CAN CONTAIN AS FEW AS THREE AND AS MANY AS FORTY LIONS.

A MALE LION'S ROAR CAN BE HEARD UP TO FIVE MILES AWAY. THE SOUND SCARES OFF INTRUDERS AND NOTIFIES OTHER MEMBERS OF THE PRIDE'S LOCATION.

FACT FILE

AVERAGE HEIGHT: 4 FEET

AVERAGE LENGTH: 5.5 FEET, 7 FEET INCLUDING TAIL

AVERAGE WEIGHT: 400 LBS

HABITAT: AFRICAN GRASSLANDS AND PLAINS, NORTHWEST INDIA.

DIET: CARNIVORE, PREDATOR.

HUNTING METHOD: LIONS STALK AND AMBUSH THEIR PREY.

BEHAVIORAL PATTERN: LIONS ARE SOCIAL BEASTS THAT LIVE IN GROUPS AND HUNT AT NIGHT. THEY RAISE THEIR YOUNG AS A COLLECTIVE. LIONS ALSO SPEND TWO-THIRDS OF THEIR TIME SLEEPING AND RESTING.

HUMAN ATTACKS PER YEAR: 550-700

THE LION HAS A TASSELED TAIL, WHICH IT OFTEN USES TO SIGNAL OTHER MEMBERS OF THE PRIDE, WARNING THEM OF DANGER.

LIONS TYPICALLY HUNT ANTELOPE, GAZELLES, RABBITS, BOAR -- ANY ANIMAL THEY CAN *FIND*. WITH THEIR **POWERFUL** LEGS AND MIGHTY *JAWS*, LIONS CAN TAKE DOWN ALMOST *ANY* ANIMAL, INCLUDING *ELEPHANTS*.

THE ONLY ANIMALS LIONS USUALLY AVOID--

--ARE *HUMANS*. LIONS

ONE OF THE **WORST** CASES OCCURRED IN THE EARLY 21ST CENTURY IN **TANZANIA**, AFRICA.

TANZANIA HAS THE **LARGEST** LION POPULATION IN AFRICA. THE GOVERNMENT DOES ITS BEST TO **PROTECT** THE BEAUTIFUL BIG CATS BY **LIMITING** LION-HUNTING.

WHEN A LION TURNS **MAN-EATER**, HOWEVER, THE AUTHORITIES DO THEIR BEST TO **TRACK** IT DOWN AND KILL IT BEFORE IT CAN **HURT** MORE PEOPLE.

ONE OF THE BIGGEST DANGERS IS THAT A LION WILL TEACH ITS **CUBS** TO HUNT **HUMANS** AS WELL.

WILD ANIMALS KILL OVER **TWO HUNDRED** PEOPLE A YEAR IN TANZANIA.

ROUGHLY A **THIRD** OF THOSE ARE FROM **LIONS**.

MOST LIONS WON'T ENTER **VILLAGES** OR OTHER LARGE CONCENTRATIONS OF **HUMANS**.

WHEN THEY **DO** ATTACK PEOPLE, THE LIONS **AMBUSH** THEM ALONG THE OUTSKIRTS OF VILLAGES, OR IN **ISOLATED** AREAS.

THIS LION'S **FIRST ATTACK** OCCURRED IN THE FALL OF 2002.

THE LION WAS **BOLDER** THAN MOST, AND HAD ATTACKED ALONG THE EDGE OF THE VILLAGE ITSELF.

IT HAD EVIDENTLY APPROACHED FROM THE NEARBY **RUFIJI RIVER**, AND ATTACKED THE **FIRST** PERSON IT FOUND.

JUDGING BY THE **PRINTS**, THE WARDENS KNEW THEY WERE LOOKING FOR A FULL-SIZED **MALE LION**. SUCH A BEAST POSED A GRAVE DANGER. THEY HAD TO FIND IT, AND **QUICKLY**.

BUT THE LION STRUCK **AGAIN** IN THE **SAME** REGION.

AND AGAIN.

AND YET AGAIN.

THE LION **CONTINUED** TO ATTACK, ALWAYS IN THE RUFIJI RIVER AREA. AND IT CONTINUED TO **ELUDE** GAME WARDENS.

TIEGLER'S GORGE

Rufiji

Mloka

Kibiti

Kikale

Mkongo

Rufiji

Ndundu

Msomeni

Utete

Mohoro

·············· border of Rufiji River floodplain

‒ ‒ ‒ ‒ border of Selous Game Reserve

0   10   20   30 KM

BY EARLY 2004 IT HAD KILLED OVER **THIRTY-FIVE** PEOPLE. THAT MADE IT THE MOST VICIOUS MAN-EATING LION **EVER!**

FINALLY, ONE MORNING IN APRIL 2004, ONE OF THE WARDENS **SPOTTED** SOMETHING!

THE MAN-EATER HAD BEEN SIGHTED AT LAST!

THE WARDENS EQUIPPED THEMSELVES QUICKLY AND CONVERGED ON THE LOCATION.

THE WARDENS WERE CAREFUL. THEY KNEW THIS LION WAS DANGEROUS.

WHAT WAS THAT?

AAAH!

RRAAARRR

BLAM

FORTUNATELY, THE WARDENS WERE **TRAINED** FOR SITUATIONS LIKE THIS. THEY COULD **REACT** EVEN WHEN THEY WERE TOO **TERRIFIED** TO THINK STRAIGHT.

AFTER TWENTY MONTHS, THEY HAD **FINALLY** STOPPED THE MAN-EATER!

WHEN THEY EXAMINED THE LION'S HEAD, RESEARCHERS FOUND IT HAD A LARGE **ABSCESS** OR **SORE** BELOW A **CRACKED MOLAR**. THE TOOTH MUST HAVE CAUSED THE LION CONSTANT **PAIN**, BUT THE PAIN WOULD HAVE INCREASED EVERY TIME IT **CHEWED**.

THE ONLY QUESTION WAS, **WHY** HAD THIS HAPPENED? WHAT HAD MADE THIS LION KILL SO **MANY** PEOPLE?

HUMAN FLESH WAS **SOFTER** THAN MOST OF THE LION'S USUAL PREY. THAT WAS PROBABLY WHY IT HAD BECOME A **MAN-EATER**.

KILLING THAT LION DIDN'T MEAN LIONS WOULD NEVER ATTACK PEOPLE **AGAIN**. BUT IT STOPPED THE PROBLEM FOR THE TIME BEING.

AND THE WARDENS WERE ALWAYS ON THE ALERT IN CASE ANOTHER LION DECIDED TO MAKE **PEOPLE** ITS FAVORITE **MEAL**.

DID YOU KNOW?

THERE ARE *SEVEN* DIFFERENT SPECIES OF LIONS: *AFRICAN, ASIATIC, AMERICAN, MOUNTAIN, CAVE, AND WHITE.*

THE *MALE* IS OFTEN REFERRED TO AS A *TOM* AND HIS MATE IS EITHER A *SHE-LION* OR A *LIONESS.* THEIR OFFSPRING, USUALLY A LITTER OF TWO, ARE KNOWN AS A *CUBS, WHELPS* OR *LIONETS.*

THE LIONESS WILL *HUNT* ON HER *OWN* TO FEED THE LITTER WHICH ARE BORN *BLIND.* WHEN THE CUBS ARE *SIX* TO *EIGHT WEEKS OLD,* THEY ARE REINTEGRATED TO THE *PRIDE* ALONG WITH THEIR MOTHER.

RHINOCEROS

THERE ARE FIVE SPECIES OF
RHINOCEROS: THE ONE-HORNED
INDIAN AND JAVAN, AND THE
TWO-HORNED SUMATRAN RHINOS
FOUND IN NORTHERN INDIA AND
SOUTHERN NEPAL, AND THE
TWO-HORNED AFRICAN SPECIES,
THE WHITE RHINO AND THE
BLACK RHINO.

THE RHINOCEROS IS STILL ILLEGALLY
HUNTED FOR ITS VALUABLE HORN IN THE
BELIEF THAT IT HAS MEDICINAL VALUE. THE
POACHING OF THESE HORNS CONTINUES
WITH INCREASING SOPHISTICATION.

RHINOS MAKE A VARIETY OF SOUNDS AND VOCALIZATIONS. THEIR SNORTS AND SQUEAKS ARE USED FOR COMMUNICATION, AS IS THEIR DUNG.

THE RHINO'S HORN IS MADE OF A MIXTURE OF COMPACTED HAIR AND KERATIN (THE SAME MATERIAL USED FOR FINGERNAILS).

FACT FILE

AVERAGE HEIGHT: 6 FEET AT THE SHOULDER

AVERAGE LENGTH: 12 FEET

AVERAGE WEIGHT: 4,000 LBS

TOP SPEED: 40 MPH

LIFESPAN: 60 YEARS

HABITAT: EASTERN AND SOUTHERN AFRICA.

DIET: HERBIVORE.

HUMAN ATTACKS PER YEAR: 12-14

ADULT AFRICAN **WHITE RHINOCEROS** MALES ARE SOLITARY ANIMALS WHICH INHABIT THE SAVANNA GRASSLANDS AND WOODLANDS IN PARTS OF SOUTHERN AFRICA.

ADULT **BULLS** HAVE TERRITORIES THAT RANGE ANYWHERE FROM 4 TO 20 SQUARE MILES, DEPENDING ON THE DENSITY OF THE RHINOCEROS POPULATION.

WHILE **YOUNG** RHINOS ARE OFTEN PREY TO BIG CATS, DOGS, CROCODILES, AND HYENAS, THE WILD, **ADULT** RHINOCEROS HAVE NO **NATURAL PREDATORS.**

EXCEPT **MAN.**

OVER THE LAST 30 YEARS, MORE THAN **90 PERCENT** OF THE WORLD'S RHINOCEROS POPULATION HAS BEEN KILLED BY HUNTERS AND POACHERS.

THOUGH NOW IN PROTECTED SANCTUARIES IN ZIMBABWE, TANZANIA, KENYA, AND OTHER COUNTRIES, THESE GREAT ANIMALS CONTINUED TO BE VICTIMIZED.

THE REASON POACHERS RISK BOTH THE LEGAL PENALTIES AND THE **DANGERS** OF HUNTING RHINOCEROS IS FOR ITS VALUABLE **HORN**.

THE HORN IS VALUED FOR ORNAMENTAL AND OTHER USES. TRADITIONAL CHINESE MEDICINE HOLDS THAT IT BATTLES FEVER AND CONVULSIONS AND POSSESSES LIFE-SAVING QUALITIES.

THEY HAVE ALSO BEEN USED SINCE THE 7TH CENTURY TO CARVE DRINKING CUPS, BOWLS, SPOONS, AND, IN THE GULF COAST, DAGGER HANDLES.

THE **JAMBIYA** IS A DAGGER TRADITIONALLY CARRIED BY MEN AND BOYS IN YEMEN. THOSE WITH HANDLES OF RHINOCEROS HORN ARE PARTICULARLY PRIZED.

·JAMBIYA·

TODAY, ARTISANS MOSTLY USE CHEAPER, LEGAL SUBSTITUTES, SUCH AS WATER BUFFALO HORN, BUT THE ILLEGAL TRADE STILL GOES ON.

BUT AS **VALUABLE** AS THE HORNS ARE, THE POACHER RISKS HIS LIFE TO PLY HIS ILLEGAL TRADE.

FEMALE AND ADOLESCENT WHITE RHINOS ARE FRIENDLY, GREETING EACH OTHER BY TOUCHING NOSES OR RUBBING HORNS ...

... BUT BULLS ARE SOLITARY, SPENDING THEIR TIME FORAGING IN TERRITORIES THEY MARK BY PHYSICAL BOUNDARIES LIKE WATERING HOLES, AS WELL AS BY SPRAYING URINE.

RHINOCEROS ARE HERBIVOROUS AND FEED ON THE TALL GRASSES OF THE SAVANNA, OFTEN SUPPLEMENTING THIS DIET BY EATING MINERAL-RICH DIRT FROM AROUND ANT MOUNDS.

BECAUSE THE GRASSES IT EATS ARE LOW IN CALORIES, RHINOS DEVOTE UP TO HALF THEIR WAKING HOURS TO GRAZING, CONSUMING MORE THAN 30 POUNDS A DAY.

THE WIDE MOUTH OF THE WHITE RHINO IS PERFECT FOR GRAZING.

UNLIKE OTHER SPECIES, THE WHITE RHINO WILL OFTEN GATHER IN SMALL HERDS, KNOWN AS A **"CRASH"** OF UP TO ABOUT A DOZEN ANIMALS.

THE WALLOW IS SHARED **PEACEFULLY** WITH MANY OTHER ANIMALS, FROM BIRDS TO WARTHOGS TO WATER BUFFALO.

WALLOWS DON'T JUST PROVIDE RHINOS WITH **WATER**, BUT ALSO A WAY TO **COOL** THEMSELVES UNDER THE BLAZING AFRICAN SUN.

MUD STIRRED UP BY THEIR HORNS AND FRONT FEET **COVERS** THE RHINOS' THICK BUT **SENSITIVE** SKIN, PROTECTING THEM FROM SUNBURN AND IRRITATING INSECT BITES!

IN FACT, IT IS DURING THE RHINO'S DAILY **WALLOWING** -- WHICH CAN LAST FOR HOURS ON HOT DAYS --THAT HE IS AT HIS MOST **VULNERABLE!**

THOUGH THEIR EYESIGHT IS WEAK, RHINOS POSSESS EXCELLENT HEARING.

SNAPP

POWERFUL MUSCLES IN THE HUMP ABOVE ITS SHOULDERS ALLOWS THE RHINO TO RAISE ITS HEAD VERY QUICKLY FROM GRAZING POSITION.

WHEN A CRASH OF RHINOCEROSES BECOMES ALARMED, THEY WILL STAND IN A CIRCLE WITH THEIR HEADS FACING OUTWARD SO THEY CAN SEE IN ALL DIRECTIONS.

A CHARGING RHINO CAN RUN AT **40 MPH** FOR SHORT BURSTS, AND IS VERY AGILE AND MANEUVERABLE FOR AN ANIMAL WHOSE REGULAR GAIT CAN BE SO SLOW AND LUMBERING.

FOR ALL ITS FEARSOME APPEARANCE AND REPUTATION, HOWEVER, RHINOCEROSES ARE MORE LIKELY TO FLEE THAN FIGHT.

BETWEEN THEMSELVES, BULLS FIGHT INFREQUENTLY, USUALLY OVER TERRITORY OR FEMALES.

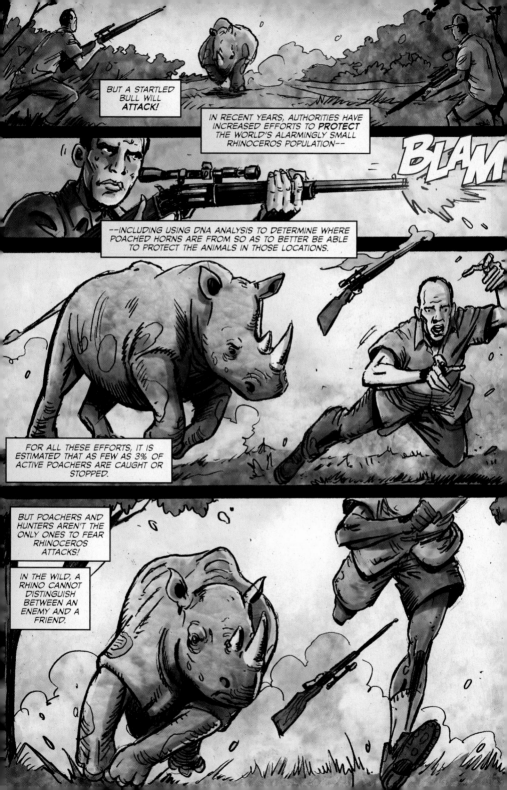

IN JANUARY 2009, A WILDLIFE PHOTOGRAPHER IN SOUTH AFRICA WAS ATTACKED BY A RHINO AS HE SNAPPED THE ANIMAL'S PICTURE FROM 90 FEET AWAY.

THE PHOTOGRAPHER WAS GORED IN HIS BACKSIDE AND THROWN THROUGH THE AIR BUT SURVIVED THE ATTACK AND RECOVERED.

SINCE 2008, THERE HAVE BEEN AT LEAST 4 DEATHS FROM RHINOCEROS ATTACKS, INCLUDING A WOMAN GATHERING FIREWOOD ALONG A RIVER, A MAN PLOWING HIS FIELDS ...

... AND A FOREST RANGER ON PATROL IN THE KAZIRANGA NATIONAL PARK IN UPPER ASSAM, WHO WAS TRAMPLED BY THE CHARGING BEAST.

BLAM BLAM

THE DANGER THESE CREATURES SOMETIMES POSE TO MAN IS REAL ... BUT SO IS THE THREAT OF EXTINCTION.

THE WORLD'S RHINOCEROS POPULATION HAS BEEN PUSHED TO THE BRINK ... BUT IS SHOWING SIGNS OF RECOVERY.

FWAM

FROM ONLY THREE RHINOS IN 1986, KENYA'S NGUILA RHINO SANCTUARY IS NOW HOME TO 70 INDIVIDUALS PROTECTED BY AN ELECTRIC FENCE.

PLACES LIKE NGUILA, ALONG WITH ZIMBABWE'S HWANGE NATIONAL PARK AND TANZANIA'S NGORONGRORO CRATER, GIVE RHINOCEROSES SAFE HAVENS IN WHICH THEY ARE THRIVING.

IT TOOK MAN ONLY A FEW, SHORT DECADES TO HUNT THE RHINOCEROS TO THE EDGE OF EXTINCTION.

THERE IS NO TELLING HOW LONG IT WILL TAKE TO REVIVE THE POPULATION OF THIS GREAT HORNED ANIMAL.

SALTWATER CROC

HAVE YOU EVER SEEN A CROCODILE SMILE? CROCODILES SWEAT THROUGH THEIR MOUTH AND LYING WITH THEIR MOUTH OPEN IS JUST A WAY TO COOL OFF.

THE SALTWATER CROC CAN TRAVEL OVER A THOUSAND KILOMETERS BY SEA BUT NEEDS DRY LAND TO REPRODUCE.

FACT FILE

AVERAGE LENGTH: 17-23 FEET

AVERAGE WEIGHT: 1,000-2,200 LBS

AVERAGE LIFESPAN: 70 YEARS

HABITAT: SOUTHEAST ASIA AND NORTHERN AUSTRALIA IN FRESH WATER SWAMPS, RIVERS, ESTUARIES AND SOMETIMES SEEN IN OPEN SEA.

DIET: PREDATOR - MAINLY FEEDS UPON MAMMALS, BIRDS AND FISH.

HUNTING METHOD: STALKS ITS PREY FOR HOURS EVEN DAYS AND USUALLY WAITS FOR ITS PREY TO GET CLOSE TO THE WATER'S EDGE BEFORE STRIKING.

HUMAN ATTACKS PER YEAR: 300-700

SALTWATER CROCS DON'T USE THEIR LEGS TO SWIM. ALL OF THE PROPULSION COMES FROM THE TAIL, WHICH MAKES UP HALF OF THE CROC'S BODY. THE TAIL ENABLES IT TO LEAP OUT OF THE WATER FROM A STATIONARY POSITION. IT IS ALSO USED AS A WEAPON AND TO STORE FAT.

...THE **SALT WATER CROCODILE.**

IN DECEMBER 2003, THREE BIKERS TREKKING THROUGH THE REMOTE TERRITORY WHERE A RECENT CYCLONE HAD **FLOODED** THE AREA FOUND OUT JUST HOW **DANGEROUS** AND **DEADLY** SALT WATER CROCS CAN BE.

CROCODILES ARE **AMBUSH** PREDATORS.

THEY STRIKE THEIR **PREY** AT THE EDGE OF THE **RIVERS, MARSHES** AND **BILLABONGS** THAT ARE FOUND THROUGHOUT AUSTRALIA.

THEY CAN GROW TO **TWENTY-FIVE FEET** IN LENGTH AND THEIR MOUTHS ARE A NIGHTMARE OF **TEETH** AND **CRUSHING FORCE.**

ONCE A CROCODILE **STRIKES** THERE IS LITTLE CHANCE OF **ESCAPE.**

IN THIS ATTACK ON THE BIKERS, THE CROCODILE SEEMED INTENT ON **PROTECTING** ITS **KILL** ...

... OR IN MAKING **ANOTHER.**

THE CROC
CONTINUED TO
TIRELESSLY STALK
THE BIKERS FOR
HOURS.

IT'S *GOT* TO BE
GONE BY NOW. I'M
GOING TO *CLIMB
DOWN.*

BE
CAREFUL.

THE HOURS PASSED WITH GRUELING SLOWNESS, GIVING THE TRAPPED BIKERS TIME TO COLLECT THEMSELVES.

ANYTIME THEY THOUGHT ABOUT CLIMBING DOWN TO GET HELP THE CROCODILE WAS *THERE*.

AFTER HOURS IN THE TREE THE BIKERS WERE FINALLY RESCUED BY *HELICOPTER*.

THEY WERE FLOWN TO A NEARBY HOSPITAL WHERE THEIR ORDEAL SOON MADE *INTERNATIONAL NEWS*.

UNFORTUNATELY, THE TRAGIC ATTACK CLAIMED THE LIFE OF THEIR FRIEND.

HIS BODY WAS NEVER RECOVERED AND THE KILLER CROC WAS NEVER IDENTIFIED.

FROM TIME TO TIME SALTWATER CROCODILES DEVELOP REPUTATIONS FOR *PROTECTING* THEIR TERRITORY.

"SWEETHEART" WAS A **HUGE** SALT WATER CROC THAT LIVED IN THE FINIS RIVER OF THE NORTHERN TERRITORY.

OVER A FIVE YEAR PERIOD IN THE LATE 1970s SWEETHEART ATTACKED OVER **FIFTEEN** SMALL BOATS.

IT IS BELIEVED THE CROC DID NOT LIKE THE **SOUND** OF THE BOATS' **MOTORS.**

IT DID NOT SEEM TO TAKE ANY INTEREST IN THE **HUMANS** IN THE BOATS AND NOT A SINGLE PERSON WAS **EVER** ATTACKED.

EVENTUALLY, SWEETHEART WAS **CAPTURED.** AFTER ITS DEATH IT WAS STUFFED AND PUT ON **DISPLAY** AT THE **DARWIN MUSEUM** IN AUSTRALIA.

IT STILL CAN BE SEEN THERE **TODAY.** A TESTAMENT TO THE SIZE AND MAJESTY OF ONE OF THE GREATEST **PREDATORS** ON OUR PLANET.

DID YOU KNOW?

IN SEPTEMBER 2011, A **ONE-TON, TWENTY-ONE FOOT** SALTWATER CROCODILE WAS CAPTURED LIVE IN THE BUNAWAN TOWNSHIP OF THE PHILIPPINES. IT REQUIRED **ONE HUNDRED PEOPLE** TO HAUL THE CROCODILE FROM THE WATER AND PLACE HIM IN AN ECOTOURISM PARK IN THE AGUSAN PROVINCE.

WILD BOAR

BOAR TUSKS GROW CONTINUALLY AND CURVE UP AND OUT, AVERAGING 3 TO 5 INCHES IN LENGTH. THEY ARE USED FOR BOTH DEFENSE AND TO ESTABLISH DOMINANCE IN THEIR HIERARCHY.

FACT FILE

AVERAGE HEIGHT: 3 FEET

AVERAGE LENGTH: 6 FEET

AVERAGE WEIGHT: 440 LBS

HABITAT: WOODLANDS IN WESTERN AFRICA, EUROPE, NORTHERN ASIA AND JAPAN, ASIA MINOR AND INDIA, INDONESIA, AND THE UNITED STATES.

DIET: OMNIVOROUS: ROOTS AND TUBERS, TO NUTS AND BERRIES.

HUNTING METHOD: WILD BOARS FORAGE FOR FOOD, DIGGING IN THE GROUND.

PREDATORS: COYOTES.

BEHAVIORAL PATTERN: WILD BOARS SPEND MUCH OF THEIR TIME SEARCHING FOR FOOD. THEY CAN DESTROY AN AREA BY DIGGING UP EVERYTHING IN SIGHT. THEY ARE VERY AGGRESSIVE -- ONCE ANGERED A BOAR WILL NOT STOP ATTACKING UNTIL IT HAS BEEN KILLED OR CAPTURED.

HUMAN ATTACKS PER YEAR: 1-2

IN ADDITION TO SUPERB HEARING, THE BOAR HAS A HIGHLY FLEXIBLE AND POWERFUL SNOUT WITH MUSCLES POWERFUL ENOUGH TO UPROOT EDIBLE PLANTS OR SENSE DANGER.

IT WAS SUMMER 2004 IN HOT, STEAMY SOUTHERN GEORGIA...

... AND MOST PEOPLE WERE **AFRAID** TO GO INTO THE WOODS.

THERE WAS A **MONSTER** IN THERE! NO ONE KNEW WHAT IT WAS, BUT IT WAS **BIG** AND **FIERCE** AND **DANGEROUS**.

BUT *CHRIS GRIFFIN* DIDN'T HAVE A *CHOICE.*

CHRIS WAS A *HUNTING GUIDE.* HE WORKED IN THE WOODS EVERY SINGLE *DAY.*

TODAY HE HAD TO GO *CLEAN UP* AFTER SOME HUNTERS HE HAD SHOWN AROUND THE DAY BEFORE. MONSTER OR *NO* MONSTER.

CHRIS WASN'T TAKING ANY *CHANCES,* THOUGH. IF THERE *WAS* A MONSTER OUT THERE, HE WOULD BE *READY* FOR IT.

THE HUNTERS HAD SET UP **DEEP** IN THE WOODS. THE **TRUCK** COULD ONLY GO SO FAR.

CHRIS HAD TO **WALK** THE REST OF THE WAY.

FINALLY, HE GOT TO THE HUNTING BLIND. THE HUNTERS HAD LEFT A **MESS**, AND PART OF HIS JOB WAS TO CLEAN UP AFTER THEM.

CHRIS WAS BUSY CLEANING WHEN HE HEARD A **NOISE** OUTSIDE IN THE **WOODS**.

HE LOOKED OUT -- AND COULDN'T **BELIEVE** HIS **EYES!**

CLEARLY, **THIS** WAS THE **MONSTER** -- AND CHRIS HAD TO KILL IT TO KEEP PEOPLE **SAFE**.

WILD BOARS WERE A **MENACE**. THEY TORE UP FARMLAND AND PASTURES AND **DESTROYED** EVERYTHING IN THEIR PATH.

THEY WERE **DANGEROUS**, TOO. BOARS WOULD **ATTACK** PEOPLE WITHOUT ANY REASON.

AND ONCE THEY GOT MAD, THEY WOULDN'T **STOP** FOR ANYTHING!

THAT WAS A **NORMAL** WILD BOAR. BUT THIS THING WAS EASILY **TWICE** AS BIG! CHRIS COULDN'T **RISK** IT HURTING ANYONE.

CHRIS TOOK CAREFUL AIM.

BOARS WERE **TOUGH**. SOMETIMES THEY KEPT COMING EVEN AFTER GETTING **SHOT**.

CHRIS KNEW THIS FIRST SHOT HAD TO BE **PERFECT**.

BLAM

IT WAS STRAIGHT TO THE **HEART!** THE BEAST FELL TO THE GROUND, **DEAD!**

SCIENTISTS LATER DUG UP THE BODY AND CONFIRMED THAT, THOUGH NOT AS BIG AS CHRIS HAD CLAIMED, THE DEAD BOAR WAS STILL *ENORMOUS.*

THEY PROVED THAT HOGZILLA HAD BEEN *REAL,* AND CHRIS HAD *KILLED* HIM.

BUT BOARS BREED *QUICKLY.* WHAT IF HOGZILLA HAD LEFT A *SON* OR TWO BEHIND IN THOSE WOODS? AND WHAT IF THEY WERE *JUST* AS BIG -- OR *BIGGER?*

A DANGEROUS WORLD...

BEASTS OF THE LAND, THE SKY AND THE OCEANS HAVE **COEXISTED** WITH MAN FOR **THOUSANDS** OF YEARS. TODAY, THOUGH, MANY OF THESE SPECIES ARE FIGHTING FOR **SURVIVAL** AS THEIR HABITATS ARE **REDUCED** OR **DESTROYED**. MANY SPECIES FACE THE DANGER OF **EXTINCTION** THROUGH POACHING AND HUNTING.

A GREATER **AWARENESS** IS REQUIRED TO UNDERSTAND THE WORLD'S **FRAGILE** ECOSYSTEMS AND REALIZE THAT OUR ACTIONS AFFECT NOT ONLY **OURSELVES** BUT **MILLIONS** OF OTHER **LIVING THINGS**.

THE WORLD'S MOST **DANGEROUS** ANIMALS ARE **FAR** FROM SAFE THEMSELVES. IN TRUTH THEY FACE THE GREATEST **DANGER**... THE DANGER OF **DISAPPEARING** FROM OUR PLANET **FOREVER**. WE MUST **REMEMBER** THAT WE **SHARE** THE EARTH WITH THESE **MAGNIFICENT** CREATURES AND WORK TO ELIMINATE THE **THREATS** WE POSE TO THEIR **EXISTENCE**... AND REALIZE HOW **LESS** MAGICAL A PLACE THE WORLD WOULD BE **WITHOUT** THEM.